Chronic Pain

....

Living by Faith When Your Body Hurts

Michael R. Emlet

New
Growth
Press

www.newgrowthpress.com

New Growth Press, Greensboro, NC 27404
Copyright © 2010 by Christian Counseling & Educational Foundation
All rights reserved. Published 2010.

Cover Design: Tandem Creative, Tom Temple, tandemcreative.net
Typesetting: Robin Black, www.blackbirdcreative.biz

ISBN-10: 1-935273-64-7
ISBN-13: 978-1-935273-64-6

Library of Congress Cataloging-in-Publication Data

Emlet, Michael R.
    Chronic pain : living by faith when your body hurts / Michael R. Emlet.
        p. cm.
    Includes bibliographical references and index.
    ISBN-13: 978-1-935273-64-6
    ISBN-10: 1-935273-64-7
    1. Chronic pain--Psychological aspects. 2. Chronic pain—Religious aspects—Christianity. 3. Chronic pain—Patients—Religious life. I. Title.
    RB127.E5225 2010
    616'.0472--dc22

                                    2010020503
Printed in China

23 22 21 20 19 18 17 16   6 7 8 9 10

Pain is Marissa's constant companion. She wakes up with it. She lives through the day with it. She goes to sleep with it. And every day is about the same. Marissa suffers with a chronic headache, which she has had for over a year. She had frequent migraine headaches throughout her teens and early twenties that put her out of commission for a day at most, but she still had been able to pursue her doctoral studies in education with enthusiasm and excellence.

Then one day her life changed. Fourteen months ago she was awakened from a deep sleep with a jackhammer exploding in her head. Despite several hospitalizations and evaluation by multiple specialists, the ultimate cause is elusive and the pain is unrelenting. Various pain medications, diets, antidepressants, regimented schedules, and more have given her only minimal relief. Now she lives at home with her parents, her doctorate on indefinite hold. Most days she forces herself to get out of bed in the morning, although she would rather stay in her room with the covers over her head. Life for Marissa has constricted like the tight bands she feels around her head.

Perhaps you, like Marissa, are experiencing chronic pain. And your life has also constricted. Almost everyone has experienced severe physical pain from illness, injury, or surgery. It hurts for awhile, and then it ends. But chronic pain is different: it doesn't stop. Like Marissa's pain, it is daily and unrelenting, the kind of bone-numbing, soul-wearying pain for which there is no end in sight. If you are experiencing that kind of pain, is it still possible for you to persevere and live out God's purposes for your life, even in the midst of your suffering? Is there grace enough? Yes, there is. God promises that his grace is sufficient for you (2 Corinthians 12:9).

But how can you experience that grace when you are suffering so much? Perhaps you are in so much pain that it's even hard for you to read this. Take your time, and work through this minibook little by little. You will find that in his Word, God has much to say to you that will give you hope, help, and comfort.

Let's begin by looking at the experience of pain and then consider how understanding God's perspective on pain and suffering can give you hope.

Your Pain Is Affected by Many Factors

You probably have already noticed that there is usually a close relationship between a painful stimulus (like touching a hot stove) and your painful experience ("Ouch!!"). But there is a difference between the body's reaction to a painful stimulus and the experience we interpret and call "pain."

Two people might touch the stove and have the exact same pain response from the nerves in their skin, but one may merely say "Ouch," and the other may scream in agony. Two children can receive the same vaccine and one will cry loudly while the other barely bats an eye. What is going on?

Understanding pain is not quite as simple as it first looks. Even acute (short-term) pain is a complex experience, influenced by many different factors. Pain receptors in your skin are set off when you touch a hot stove or get a shot. Nerve fibers carry pain messages to your brain. That is the physical aspect of pain. But there are many other factors that contribute to the heightening or the lessening of your pain experience. Your pain will be affected by your cultural background, anticipation of the pain, and previous experience with pain, along with how emotional you are and how you think about pain. The interplay of these various factors is even more complex in chronic pain.

But knowing that pain is more than a physical experience should give you hope. If your pain is not set in stone physiologically (and secular pain theorists know it is not), then you can have hope for not just coping with pain, but for growing more like Christ in the midst of pain.

God's Perspective on Pain

How can you grow more like Christ even when your body hurts? It starts with understanding God's perspective on pain. Because we are both physical and spiritual beings (Genesis 2:7; Ecclesiastes 12:7), we experience all of life in both physical and spiritual ways. How does this relate to the issue of pain?

Pain is a physical problem because the fall of Adam and Eve into sin had definite physical consequences, including pain and physical death (Genesis 2:17; 3:16–17; 5:5). In the Bible God speaks about the universal experience of physical pain (Job 33:19; Ecclesiastes 2:23).

But pain is also a spiritual problem. We see this in two ways:

1. *Physical pain entered the world because of sin, so the experience of physical pain is a direct effect of the disobedience of Adam and Eve.* This doesn't mean that your pain is tied directly to your personal sin, but it does mean that your pain must be understood in the larger context of sin and the full redemption (physical and spiritual) that Jesus brings. So persevering in the midst of chronic pain involves not only pursuing physical solutions for pain control, but also living in light of the truth that Jesus' kingdom has been established and that the full benefits of redemption involve the end of pain, suffering, sin, and death (Luke 4:38–40; 13:10–13; Revelation 21:4). Jesus himself endured the agony of the cross for the ultimate joy—the anticipated victory of his resurrection—set before him (Hebrews 12:2).

2. *Pain is a spiritual issue because the physical pain you are experiencing forces you to respond either rightly*

or sinfully. You can interpret and respond to your chronic pain with a God-shaped perspective or with a human perspective. We most naturally respond to pain with a self-oriented human perspective. Here are a few such responses to pain you might have already experienced:

- I must get rid of this pain at all costs.
- God must be punishing me.
- God owes me an easier life. ☆
- I can't do what God has called me to do because of this unrelenting pain. ☆

These responses lead to feelings of fear, anxiety, anger, bitterness, self-pity, and despair that can make your pain experience worse.

But can you see how the following God-centered beliefs and attitudes can change your experience of pain?

- God provides the resources I need each day to persevere. *all sufficient grace*

BORE OUR PAIN

- He understands the depths of pain.
- I don't understand why God won't take away the pain, but I lean on his faithfulness and love to me through Jesus.

These responses can lead to joy, hope, perseverance, and others-centeredness in the midst of your pain. Our belief or unbelief in the character and promises of God will alter our pain experience for better or for worse.

Expect to Groan in This Life

Jesus' kingdom has been established through his life, death, resurrection, and ascension (Acts 2:22–36). Jesus experienced physical pain and spiritual alienation in order to overcome physical pain and death and the eternal consequences of sin (Hebrews 2:9–18). We live in the time period between his first and second comings, when the blessings of his redemption are *already* present but *not yet* fully realized (Ephesians 1:3–14; Hebrews 2:8; Revelation 21—22).

This is why Paul speaks of suffering as a hallmark of the Christian's life (Romans 8:16–25). "Groaning" and "glory" describe the experience of life this side of Jesus' second coming. When pain is unrelenting, you groan. Although you have the firstfruits of the Spirit, you acutely experience your body's "bondage to decay" (Romans 8:21). Yet the Holy Spirit living in you is God's down payment guaranteeing what is to come; he gives you the strength to persevere in faith until you experience the redemption of your body at the resurrection (Ephesians 1:14).

Suffering Is Purposeful

Another important biblical perspective on chronic pain is that suffering is purposeful. In the midst of your pain you may respond, "I have yet to see anything good come of this constant suffering; it has ruined my life and sapped my joy." But don't let your experience speak louder than the words of Scripture. Don't let your experience dictate to you what is true about God and his character. Instead, let what is true about God and his purposes, as laid out in the Bible, reframe and reinterpret your painful experience.

The Bible says again and again that God is up to something remarkable in allowing you to suffer. His project is a big one—he is transforming and perfecting your character (Romans 5:1–5; James 1:2–8; 1 Peter 1:3–9). Knowing that God is at work in you for your good will strengthen your will to persevere, even on the days when you are tempted to choose an imperfect character over the purifying presence of pain.

He who began a good work will carry it to completion.

Practical Strategies for Change

depends on the da[...]

What is your ultimate goal in dealing with chronic pain? Is it to remove pain or to redeem pain? Is it to take away pain or to transform pain? Isn't it both? Certainly you should pray for relief from pain. Take steps to relieve your pain—consult with doctors, go to physical therapy, try legal medications and any other lawful pain-control methods. But realize that these steps may or may not be helpful.

? 0

Expectation ☆ Management

Remember that Scripture speaks about the benefit of experiencing pain and suffering as well as the benefit of relieving suffering. Scripture ultimately <u>holds</u> these <u>truths</u> together in Jesus Christ. If your ultimate goal and hope is that God will redeem your pain experience, so that you might better reflect him and be better equipped to minister comfort to others who are hurting, then you can <u>be absolutely confident</u> that God intends

hope?

to transform your pain in that very way.

Paul says this about what God is up to in our lives: "We know that in all things God works for the good of those who love him, who have been called according to his purpose" (Romans 8:28). When you read all of Romans 8, you will notice that this famous verse directly follows Paul's discussion of suffering and groaning. Paul also says that he is "confident of this, that he who began a good work in you will carry it on to completion until the day of Christ Jesus" (Philippians 1:6). Your pain and suffering will not stop the good work that God began in you and is bringing to completion.

PART of the plan. Not an interruption

Develop a Christ-Centered Gaze on Your Pain

Did you know that your suffering occurs alongside of Christ's? *Your* life story (including pain) is embedded in *his* story (including pain). Your suffering, which at first glance might appear to be a completely isolated subjective experience, is actually a participation in the very sufferings of Christ (2 Corinthians 1:5; Philippians 3:10; 1 Peter 4:12–13).

Consider Paul's amazing statement: "Now I rejoice

I carry with me in this body the death of Christ that the life of Christ might be made manifest.

13

in what was suffered for you, and I fill up in my flesh what is still lacking in regard to Christ's afflictions, for the sake of his body, which is the church" (Colossians 1:24). Paul is not saying that your sufferings add anything to Christ's work on the cross. There's nothing deficient about Jesus' suffering and death. He is saying that there is a purposeful link between the sufferings of Christ and your own suffering.

Your connection with Jesus means that your identity is bigger than that of a chronic pain sufferer. Your long-term experience of pain, or any other chronic illness, has the potential to define who you are. But read what Paul says: "If we are children, then we are heirs—heirs of God and co-heirs with Christ, if indeed we share in his sufferings in order that we may also share in his glory" (Romans 8:17). Paul is saying that your suffering actually confirms your identity as a child of God. It does not undermine that identity, even though it sometimes feels that way in the midst of your pain. This perspective reminds you that as you suffer, you suffer *in Christ.* Your life (both suffering and, ultimately, glory) is intimately connected with his life.

Use the Bible to Give Voice to Your Suffering

Nowhere does Scripture say to a suffering person, "Thou shalt have a stiff upper lip!" In the middle of your chronic pain you are not called to live as a stoic before God or others. How can you give voice to your suffering in a way that's not self-indulgent? Go to the Psalms, especially Psalms 13; 77; and 88. There you can add your voice to those who have cried out to God as they were suffering in distressing and confusing circumstances. God wants you to wrestle honestly with him about the confusion and pain in your life. But don't stop there. Imitate the psalmists who struggled like you, but as they struggled, they continued to anchor their hope in the character, work, and promises of God. Their hope finds its fulfillment in the Lord Jesus Christ. Because he was forsaken, you won't be forsaken in your distress (Psalm 22).

School Yourself in the Hope of the Resurrection

It is easy for the average person who does not experience chronic illness or pain to think about the hope of the resurrection in some detached, far-off way. But as you struggle with chronic pain, ask God to make the hope of the resurrection tangible, real, and meaningful. As you acutely feel the decay of your body, let God use that to make you long for the day of resurrection when you will stand perfected, body and spirit, before the living God. Because Jesus himself suffered, died, was buried, and experienced bodily resurrection, you can be sure that, one day, you will be resurrected with a new body (1 Corinthians 15:20–28). Remind yourself of these truths every morning. Read often the account of Jesus' resurrection in Matthew 28, Mark 16, Luke 24, and John 20. Meditate on the hope of the resurrection expressed by Paul in 1 Corinthians 15 and Philippians 3:10–11. Remember that as you suffer with Christ, you will also be raised with Christ.

Look for Ways to Love Others

Chronic pain, like all suffering, tempts us to withdraw, to turn inward, and to place our needs above the needs of others. Even as a chronic pain sufferer, the second great commandment—"Love your neighbor as yourself"—still applies to you (Matthew 22:39; Mark 12:31). God still calls you (and equips you!) to be an instrument of his truth, grace, and love in the lives of people around you. The actions prompted by this love will be different for you as you deal with chronic pain, but that doesn't mean you can't love others. Ask God to give you a vision for loving those around you in specific ways, even if the acts of love seem like small steps. Here are some suggestions to help you start the brainstorming process:

- Keep a prayer journal that includes intercession for the needs of your family, friends, and members of your church—and then actually pray.
- Write a brief note of encouragement to a struggling person.
- Seek to be fully attentive to your child as she recounts her day in school (though you may be tempted toward irritability and distraction due to your pain).
- Fold the laundry.
- Prepare or buy a meal for a shut-in.

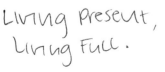

Living Present,
Living Full.

Learn How to Respond to Those Who Don't Understand

One of the challenges you (and the body of Christ) face is that, unlike people who have had an injury causing acute pain, people who struggle with chronic pain often don't show any outward signs of the severity of the struggle (e.g. a cast, crutches, bandages, a wheelchair, etc.). Someone experiencing chronic pain may look "normal" to others. Often, this creates a disconnect between your experience and their experience of you and your struggle.

How often have you heard in one way or another, "C'mon it can't be that bad, can it? Just trust God to give you strength, and then step out in faith"? There are many temptations you face when others respond to you like this. Probably you have experienced some of these:

- Withdrawing in hopelessness ("They'll never understand, so why bother?")
- Going on an angry offensive ("How dare you lecture me about something you know nothing about! Let me give you a picture of the living hell I endure day after day....")

- Living as a stoic, compartmentalizing (if that's even possible!) your experience of chronic pain from other aspects of corporate church life

Ask God to help you avoid the extremes of self-indulgence or stoicism. Chronic pain is not your identity—either to be nursed in silent hopelessness or defended in anger. But it *is* part of how God is shaping you as a person, and so it must shape in some way your interaction with others. Here are a few suggestions that may foster a deeper understanding between you and others who do not share your experience of chronic pain:

- Answer questions in a non-defensive way. "I appreciate your concerns about my absences from Sunday school. Could I share a bit with you regarding the difficulties I face in the mornings to get ready, due to my pain?"
- Speak with the leaders of your church regarding your specific challenges (and more generally, the challenges of anyone who experiences chronic illness). This might encourage a shepherding plan that addresses not only

acute illnesses and hospitalizations, but also chronic illnesses.

- Assess how much your pain experience dominates your conversations (Ephesians 4:29).
- Inquire genuinely about the struggles of others.
- Give a talk about the experience of chronic pain to educate others in your congregation.
- If you're not a chronic pain sufferer, take the time to enter into the sufferings of your neighbor (Romans 12:15). Ask, listen, and pray! Then ask again soon!

WHEN OTHERS COMPLAIN?

Consider Options for Medical (Physical) Treatment of Chronic Pain

Entire textbooks have been written on this topic. As I mentioned earlier, by all means pursue medical and physical strategies for the relief and improvement of your pain, while not allowing your goal of pain relief to become an enslaving (and often elusive) idol.

Listed below are some (of many!) treatments that might help reduce your chronic pain. Some of these strategies are more helpful for a specific type or location of pain, such as the low back.

- Anti-inflammatory medications such as ibuprofen or naproxen
- Narcotic medications such as codeine, morphine, or synthetically created opioids (usually for refractory pain)
- Antiepileptic drugs (particularly helpful for chronic pain from damaged nerves—"neuropathic pain")
- Antidepressants (to directly modulate pain pathways, not necessarily to treat depressive symptoms; also particularly helpful for neuropathic pain)
- Physical therapy—although it may seem paradoxical, exercise/movement tends to improve pain control, particularly in non-neuropathic pain such as chronic arthritis
- Occupational therapy
- Epidural or spinal injections
- Spinal cord stimulation or peripheral nerve field stimulation

- Muscle relaxants
- TENS (transcutaneous electrical nerve stimulation)
- Acupuncture
- Botanical medicine (herbs)

Note that use of any of these methods is a wisdom issue, to be prayerfully decided by you based upon the input of your physician(s) and trusted family and friends who can help bring a biblical worldview to bear upon these treatment decisions. If you are a smoker, now is a good time to quit! Nicotine use is associated with *increased* pain levels.

Expect successes and failures as your regimen of treatment is tailored to you. If your pain seems particularly severe or unmanageable, consider seeking help at a regional or university hospital pain center.

These steps of faith I have suggested will not be easy. But remember, you are not alone. Your Savior Jesus Christ, who experienced the path of pain and suffering before you, has given you his Spirit—the very presence of Jesus!—to empower you and comfort you in your suffering (2 Corinthians 1:3–5). Know that God intends, despite your bodily pain, to renew you inwardly day by day (2 Corinthians 4:16). And although it may not feel like it, that is glory in the making (2 Corinthians 4:10, 17).

Simple, Quick, Biblical

Advice on Complicated Counseling Issues
for Pastors, Counselors, and Individuals

MINIBOOK
CATEGORIES

- Personal Change
- Marriage & Parenting
- Medical & Psychiatric Issues
- Women's Issues
- Singles
- Military

USE YOURSELF | GIVE TO A FRIEND | DISPLAY IN YOUR CHURCH OR MINISTRY

New Growth Press

Go to **www.newgrowthpress.com** or call **336.378.7775** to
purchase individual minibooks or the entire collection.
Durable acrylic display stands are also available to house
the minibook collection.